# Say What?!

Clare Luther · Emma Randall

10 Publishing
a division of 10ofthose.com

Say what?!

Take a Look!

God writes his story in a book.

GENESIS 1:31A

God looked at everything he had made, and it was very good.

The Bible tells us all about God.
God is the Creator of the universe.
He has made everything in it.
He is King of all he has made.

God spoke, and in six days he made everything: day and night, the sky, sun, moon and stars, the sea, rivers and streams, land, plants, fruit and trees, and all the creatures in the sky, in the water and on land. But God saved the **best** until last. From dust on the ground, he made man and woman in his likeness.

On day seven God rested from creating. God said everything was very good and he was pleased. The world was finished and **full** of life, just as God planned, and it was perfect!

Say what?!

It is true!

God knows all about me and you.

PSALM 139:1

Lord, you have examined me.
You know all about me.

God knows how our planet works best because he made it. God knows about the seasons and the weather and about every plant, fruit and tree.

God knows about all the creatures on land, in the water and in the sky. God knows about each person, including you and me, because he made us.

Every day, in every moment, God keeps life going everywhere. God is Creator and King of **all** life. God loves each one of us very much and he wants to be our friend. Fantastic!

Say what?!

We can't hear!

We've got
a finger in
each ear.

JEREMIAH 32:33

They turned their backs to me. I tried to teach them again and again. But they wouldn't listen to me. I tried to correct them, but they wouldn't listen.

In the Bible, God tells us the best way to live.
He says it is for us to know him and to love him.
To know and to love God brings us great joy!

He also tells us to love each other, to be kind to others,
to tell the truth, and to care for the world we live in.

But we don't always do this.
We ignore God and put ourselves first.
We make ourselves king.

This means sometimes we don't care for the world we live in. Sometimes we don't love each other; we are unkind, we lie and we hurt other people. When we don't listen to God, life is messy. Oh no!

Say what?!

God knows best!

He sees when we get in a mess.

ROMANS 3:23

All people have sinned and are not good enough for God's glory.

When we ignore God, it's like we are saying, "I'm not listening, I'm in charge!" God calls this sin. It's impossible to live God's way if we are not listening to him.

God is perfect and we are not. Because we sin, we cannot be friends with a God who is perfect. There is nothing you or I can do to fix this.

But God loves each one of us so much
that he makes a way for us to be his friends.
Thank you God!

Say what?!

There's a plan!

God's Son comes to Earth as a man.

ROMANS 5:8

But Christ died for us while we were still sinners. In this way God shows his great love for us.

God had a rescue plan. He sent his Son down from Heaven to Earth. God's Son became a real man called Jesus. The Bible tells us lots of stories about Jesus's power so that we can be certain that he is God.

Jesus died on a cross for our sins.
Jesus took the punishment we deserve for not
living God's way. Jesus died instead of us.

Jesus didn't stay dead.
After three days, he rose from
the dead because he is God.

God is more powerful than death. Jesus is alive again. Death is not the end. Amazing! Jesus lives forever.

Say what?!

Just believe!

God's love is for us to receive.

MARK 1:14B–15B

Jesus went into Galilee and preached the Good News from God. Jesus said... "Change your hearts and lives and believe the Good News!"

Jesus's death means we can now be friends with God and God can be our King. Jesus came to put things right between us and God. Jesus came to forgive, to rescue and to save us. Wow!

When we say sorry to God for not listening to him and believe that Jesus died for us, we are forgiven for our sins. We can be friends with God now and we look forward to living with God as our King forever. Jesus helps us to live the best way we can on Earth and be excited about our home in Heaven.

Because of Jesus, we can be part of God's family. We can read the Bible and hear what God has to say. We can talk to God anytime in prayer. We can sing songs praising God. We have God's Spirit with us every minute of every day. We can talk with our family and friends about God. We have a forever life with God. Hooray!

Say what?!

Start again!

Say sorry,
yes Jesus,
Amen.

EPHESIANS 2:8

I mean that you have been saved by grace because you believe. You did not save yourselves. It was a gift from God.

This is the **best** news ever! We can know the love and forgiveness of Jesus when we say sorry and ask him to be our King and Rescuer. Forever friends with God and a forever life with God. We are never alone. Yes! Thank you, Jesus. Amen!

# Prayer Time

Thank you,

Sorry,

Please.

Dear God,
Thank you that you know me.
Thank you for loving me so much that you sent your Son, Jesus, to Earth to die for me and save me. I have done things and I have said things that are wrong. I am sorry. Forgive me when I do not live your way.
Please help me to have you as King and Rescuer of my life.
In Jesus's name,
Amen.

# Rhyme Time

Say what?!
Take a look!
God writes his
story in a book.

Say what?!
It is true!

God knows
all about me
and you.

Say what?!
We can't hear!
We've got a finger
in each ear.

Say what?!
God knows best!
He sees when we
get in a mess.

Say what?!
There's
a plan!

God's Son
comes to Earth
as a man.

Say what?!
Just believe!
God's love is for
us to receive.

Say what?!
Start again!
Say sorry,
yes Jesus, Amen.

JOHN 3:16

For God loved the world so much that he gave his only Son. God gave his Son so that whoever believes in him may not be lost, but have eternal life.

ISBN: 978-1-915705-06-8

Published by 10Publishing, a division of 10ofThose Limited, Tomlinson Road, Leyland, Lancs, PR25 2DY, England
info@10ofthose.com www.10ofthose.com

Written by Clare Luther
Illustrated by Emma Randall
Designed by Diane Warnes

1 3 5 7 9 10 8 6 4 2